Psalm 121:
Looking to the Hills

Barry A. Allen

Copyright © 2018 Barry Alexander Allen

All rights reserved.

ISBN-10: 1723110027

ISBN-13: 978-1723110023

All Scripture references are from the King James Version of the Bible

For

Rev. Ken and Rev. Angela Nelson

Contents

PART I – PSALM 121:1-2. 9

PART II – PSALM 121:3-4. 21

PART III – PSALM 121:5-6. 35

PART IV – PSALM 121:7-8. 57

Psalm 121:1-8

"I will lift up mine eyes unto the hills, from whence cometh my help. My help cometh from the Lord, which made heaven and earth. He will not suffer thy foot to be moved: he that keepeth thee will not slumber. Behold, he that keepeth Israel shall neither slumber nor sleep. The Lord is thy keeper: the Lord is thy shade upon thy right hand. The sun shall not smite thee by day, nor the moon by night." The Lord shall preserve thee from all evil: he shall preserve thy soul. The Lord shall preserve thy going out and thy coming in from this time forth, and even for evermore."

PART I – PSALM 121:1-2

Chapter 1 – Psalm 121:1-2

"I will lift up mines eyes unto the hills, from whence cometh my help. My help cometh from the Lord, which made heaven and earth."

Trials, Difficulties, and the Promise of God's Presence, Power, and Help

We all face trials and difficulties in our lives. All persons, regardless of their station in life, wealth, ability, and talents, periodically encounter problems as they journey through the wonderful experience we call life. No one is exempt from pain, hardship, grief, and disappointment. This was true for the Psalmist who penned Psalm 121, and it is true for us Christians today. We live in a culture that is not consistently friendly towards Christianity, and we are sometimes persecuted or left out due to our allegiance to Christ. Jesus tells us this in John 15:17-19 where he says:

> These things I command you, that ye love one another. If the world hate you, ye know that it hated me before it hated you. If ye were of the world, the world would love his own: but because ye are not of the world, but I have chosen you out of the world, therefore the world hateth you.

Just as the world rejected and persecuted Jesus, it will also reject and persecute those who follow and worship him. We will also have other problems which are common to all men and women like sickness, grief, pain, disappointment, heartache, ailments, and suffering. Psalm 121 gives us guidance on how to deal with the trials of life by looking to God for help instead of looking around for answers in the secular realm of this world. The Psalmist encourages us to "look up" instead of "looking around," and we will find help in our time of need if we look to God for help instead of looking for help among the so called "experts" in this fallen world which rejects our Lord and his teachings. Indeed, we sometimes need an "expert" to help us get through a situation or season in our lives, but we can usually find a Christian who has the training and expertise to help us through these difficult times. Jesus assures us that we will face difficulties by stating: "…In the world ye shall have tribulation: but be of good cheer; I have overcome the world" (John 16:33).

I recently discovered a powerful truth about trials and difficulties, and one of the great blessings contained in the common human experience of heartache and pain. No matter how little we may have in common with others, we all share the common experience of difficulty and heartache. We may not have anything else in common with someone, but we all share common ground in that we all know what it means to face trials and difficulties. This gives us something in common even if we have nothing else in common, and we can find a place where we can connect if we open ourselves up to sharing with one another the hardships of our shared human experiences of loss, grief, pain, sickness, suffering, and hardship. Then, we are blessed with the realization that we are not all that different, and we have more in common than we initially thought. A good analogy is the fact that if we are cut, we all bleed red blood. All of us have red blood, and we all bleed red blood if we are injured or suffer a laceration. The color of our blood is something that we all have in common, and our one color of blood points to the fact that we all share the common experience of pain and suffering when our blood is shed or we face other trials and difficulties in life. This gives us a place to unite and to be together as we walk together through the painful and difficult experiences of life. We are not alone. We have each other, and we have God. Sure, we sometimes need the experts such as doctors, dentists, mechanics, carpenters, and so on, but we need to consult God through the Word, prayer, and public worship consistently so that he may guide us in our decisions and direct us through the challenges that come our way in life.

This is one of the fundamental messages of Psalm 121. In v. 1, he says: "I will lift up mine eyes unto the hills, from whence cometh my help" (Psalm 121:1). Notice, the Psalmist says he will "lift up" his eyes. He is making the decision to "look up" instead of "looking around." This is one of the fundamental keys to managing and navigating the difficulties of life. We need to "look up" in faith to God instead of "looking around" at our circumstances. This is Biblical advice, and it is in part what Jesus talks about in Matthew 6:33 where he says: "…seek ye first the kingdom of God, and his righteousness; and all these things shall be added unto you." This verse is located in Jesus' powerful teaching where he encourages not to worry but to trust in God. (See Matthew 6:25-34) If we consistently "look around" at our circumstances, we run the risk of being overwhelmed by them or thinking too much about them. This can lead us to catastrophic thinking fueled by fear which is in opposition to the optimistic and hopeful thinking that is rooted and grounded in our faith in a loving and benevolent heavenly Father who loves us so much "...that he gave his only begotten Son, that whosoever believeth in him should not perish, but have everlasting life" (John 3:16).

Trusting the Creator Instead of the Creation: The Beauty, Power, and Strength of Believing and Trusting in a Loving and Giving God

In Psalm 23:1, the Psalmist says: "The Lord is my shepherd; I shall not want." This is one of the greatest verses of Scripture in the entire Bible, and it is a great affirmation of faith in our loving, giving, and always present God. Frequently, we read over this verse so fast, or quote it so fast, that we forget to pause and celebrate the truth contained in it. The verse means that we have everything because we have God, our Creator, and he loves us and cares for us forever. God's great love for us is evident in that he "...commendeth his love toward us, in that, while we were yet sinners, Christ died for us" (Romans 5:8).

We lift up our eyes to a hill called Mt. Calvary, and we find hope and strength in our time of need. This is in part what Jesus speaks of in John 12:32 where he states: "And I, if I be lifted up from the earth, will draw all men unto me." In vv. 1-2 of Psalm 121, the Psalmist makes the point that he will look to the Creator for help and not to the creation. As he looks at the mountains, he knows his help does not come from this world which God created, but his help comes from the almighty One who created this world. It is interesting to note that the Psalmist makes the conscience decision to let the mountains be a source of inspiration instead of an obstacle in his way. Instead of viewing the hills as something to be climbed over to get to the other side, he instead looks at their beauty and is inspired that they reflect the power, glory, and strength of the One who formed them and put them in their place on the earth. The Psalmist chooses to allow the creation to inspire him to have faith in the strength and power of the Creator instead of viewing creation as something man must navigate and overcome to get to his destination. This is in part what it means to "...walk by faith, not by sight..." (2 Corinthians 5:7), and this is in part what it means to trust in our God and Savior, Jesus Christ, who promises "...All power is given unto me in heaven and in earth....and, lo, I am with you always, even unto the end of the world...." (Matthew 28:18, 20)

In v. 2, the Psalmist answers the rhetorical question of v. 1 by stating: "My help cometh from the Lord, which made heaven and earth" (Psalm

121:2). While looking at the beauty of the mountains and God's creation, the Psalmist is reminded that God is good and God is at work in the world. This prompts the Psalmist to have faith instead of fear as he looks at his future and speculates about the challenges he will face in the days and years ahead. The glorious beauty and the massive size of the enormous mountains remind him of God's great goodness and immense power, and this inspires him to face the future knowing that he has God's power and strength on his side. The Psalmist knows that the One who created the mountains and put them in place is the same God who will come to him in his time of need, so he, like the apostle Paul, rejoices in the truth that: "…If God be for us, who can be against us?" (Romans 8:31)

PART II – PSALM 121:3-4

Chapter 2 – Psalm 121:3-4

"He will not suffer thy foot to be moved: he that keepeth thee will not slumber. Behold, he that keepeth Israel shall neither slumber nor sleep."

The Great Faithfulness of our God Who Never Blinks, Turns Away, Slumbers, or Sleeps

One of the great things about being a son or daughter of God and being a theologian is that we continue to discover amazing things about God and ourselves. Every Christian is a theologian in that every Christian has a relationship with God through Jesus and the Holy Spirit. And, every Christian talks or writes or communicates to others about that relationship using words. This is what a theologian is. A theologian is someone who speaks or writes about God using words. Therefore, all of us born-again and believing Christians are "theologians." Then, there are also those of us who are "professional" or "trained" theologians. We are your preachers, seminary and university professors, religious school teachers, authors, writers, journalists, chaplains, counselors, missionaries, and evangelists who earn our living speaking and teaching about God, the Bible, church history, theology, and spirituality.

I am in this latter category of "theologians," and it is a great blessing to be among those who speak and teach about God "full-time." One of the things I particularly enjoy about it is the fact that some of the greatest discoveries I "unearth" as a digging and excavating theologian are some of the most basic truths like the one we are about to look at in vv. 3-4 of Psalm 121. God never gets tired, and God never sleeps. He is always awake and watching, and he is always looking out for and caring for those who trust in him. Now, in order for this to have the power and impression upon us that it is suppose to, we need to pause and recall exactly what it is like to be completely exhausted. Perhaps you don't have to pause and remember because you had a very long day today, and you are reading this as you wind down to turn in for the night. Whichever is the case, we can easily remember and agree that we are not good at being efficient or watchful, or good at keeping an eye on or watching out for someone or something, when we are really tired.

The Psalmist tells us in vv. 3-4 of Psalm 121 that God never gets tired, and he never stops watching out for and caring for us. He watches over us 24 hours a day 365 days a year, and he never even blinks or misses watching over us for even a second. This is such a basic theological truth, but it is so profound. Only our heavenly Father can watch over us this perfectly. Through the birth, life, ministry, death, and resurrection of Jesus Christ, God came to be with us and to be our Emmanuel, God with us, as the angel explains to Joseph in his dream:

> Behold, a virgin shall be with child, and shall bring forth a son, and they shall call his name Emmanuel, which being interpreted is, God with us. Then Joseph being raised from sleep did as the angel of the Lord had bidden him, and took unto him his wife: And knew her not till she had brought forth her firstborn son; and he called his name JESUS.
> (Matthew 1:23-25)

God came to be with us incarnate in the Jewish flesh of a Baby Boy named Jesus, and this Baby Boy grew up and went to a cross where his broken body and shed blood reconciled us to his and our heavenly Father for now and forever. The great chasm that sin had created, causing us to be separated from God and his kingdom, has been bridged by the broken body and shed blood of Christ. This is what salvation is. Salvation is being saved from the consequences of our sins which ultimately is spiritual death and eternal separation from God. Since Christ paid the penalty for our sins at the cross, our sin-debt has been paid, and we can now walk and talk with our perfectly holy and righteous God. Those who trust in Christ are "justified" and declared "not guilty" by God. We are not "not guilty," but we are declared "not guilty" by God. This enables us to be in God's presence and makes it possible for us to be reconciled to and live our lives with God both now and forever. The broken body and shed blood of Christ enables us to have God present in every moment and every day in every year of our lives, and:

> He will not suffer thy foot to be moved: he that keepeth thee will not slumber. Behold, he that keepeth Israel shall neither slumber nor sleep.
> (Psalm 121:3-4)

God Keeps Us from Falling and is always Loving, Giving, Caring, and Protecting

In John 3:16, we see the heart, mind, and will of God as we read: "For God so loved the world, that he gave his only begotten Son, that whosoever believeth in him should not perish, but have everlasting life." Here, in this iconic verse of Scripture, we see that the heart of God is filled with love for all persons in the world. God "...loved the world... [and] ...gave his only begotten Son... [so that] ...whosoever believeth..." could be saved and have eternal life. (John 3:16) No one is excluded in God's kingdom, and Jesus' atoning death on the cross made salvation possible for "...whosoever believeth in him should not perish but have everlasting life" (John 3:16). Unfortunately, only those who accept the gift of salvation by accepting Christ as their Lord and Savior, trusting completely in his atoning work at the cross as the only payment for their sins, will actually receive the gift of salvation and everlasting life. However, one drop of Jesus' blood is more than enough to cover every sin ever committed, or that will ever be committed in the future, by sinful men and women. His blood is this powerful because his blood is the blood of God, shed by the Second Person of the Holy Trinity, God the Son, Jesus Christ. It is the pure and holy and unblemished blood of almighty God incarnate in the Jewish flesh of Jesus the Christ, the God-man, who is 100% God and 100% man. The death of no other would even scratch the surface of atoning for all of the wicked things men and women have done throughout the annals of human history, but one tiny drop of the blood of the Son of God, who is also God the Son, is more than enough to cover all of the the sins ever committed, and that ever will be committed, by sinful men and women in this sinful and fallen world. This is the gift God gave at the cross motivated by his love for the world and all of the sinful men and women living in it. I frequently tell people that the "…whosoever…" of John 3:16 is one of my very favorite words in the Bible. Sometimes, they ask why, and I say because I am so thankful that the "…whosoever…" of John 3:16 includes me.

In John 3:16, we also see the mind and the will of God. We see that God loves sinners and he thinks of them and longs for their return to him. All three of the wonderful parables of Luke 15 make it very clear that God loves and thinks of sinners and that it is his will that they return home to him or be found by him. (See Luke 15:1-32) God is like the shepherd who leaves the 99 sheep to go and find the 1 that is lost. (Like 15:1-7) And, God is like the woman who continually sweeps her house searching for the coin she lost. (Luke 15:8-10) And, God is also like the loving father who awaits and longs for the return of his sinful and rebellious son. (Luke 15:11-32)

God's mind is on sinners, and he seeks them and waits for them. God paid a very high price to make a way for sinners to be reunited with him, and it is his will that all sinners receive the gift of salvation and be reconciled to him. Sadly, only those who accept the gift by trusting in the broken body of shed blood of Christ will actually receive the gift of salvation, but this doesn't change the fact that one drop of Jesus' blood is so perfectly pure, and perfectly holy, that it covers every sin ever committed by every sinner in the history and future of humanity. In John 3:16, it is evident that God's heart loves sinners, and his mind thinks and cares for sinners, and his will is that lost sinners be found and reconciled to him. If we want to reach the lost for Christ, we need to have hearts and minds that love and think about sinners, and our will needs to be in line with God's will as we pray, work, give, care, love, and welcome sinners into the kingdom of God. Indeed, God has given us the Great Commission, and he calls us to go and: "…teach all nations…" about the Good News of salvation and the Great Commandments of Jesus Christ. (Matthew 28:16-20) And, God has entrusted us with the ministry of reconciliation as Paul points out in 2 Corinthians 5:19-21 where he states:

> …God was in Christ, reconciling the world unto himself, not imputing their trespasses unto them; and hath committed unto us the word of reconciliation. Now then we are ambassadors for Christ, as though God did beseech you by us: we pray you in Christ's stead, be ye reconciled to God. For he hath made him to be sin for us, who knew no sin; that we might be made the righteousness of God in him.

We celebrate that the God of John 3:16 is the God of Psalm 121:3-4, and he keeps us and never slumbers or sleeps. (Psalm 121:4) Men and women of this world will fall asleep on us, look away from us, abandon us, and blink their eyes and lose sight of us. They are just not capable of loving, caring, thinking, and willing the best for us as God does. And, God promises us that he will never leave nor forsake us, he will be with us always, his goodness and mercy will follow us all the days of our lives, and we will dwell in his house both now and forever. (Hebrews 13:5, Matthew 28:20, and Psalm 23:6)

PART III – PSALM 121:5-6

Chapter 3 – Psalm 121:5-6

"The Lord is thy keeper: the Lord is thy shade upon thy right hand. The sun shall not smite thee by day, nor the moon by night."

The Lord Protects Us and Watches Over Us as We Come and Go and Work and Play

Here in Psalm 121:5-6, we have a profound and glorious promise that God watches over us as we come and go and work and play in this hostile and fallen world. Many Christians go daily to jobs that are downright dangerous such as being a police officer, a sheriff deputy, or serving in the armed forces. Also, many Christians go to work daily working in construction, fighting the elements, building houses and skyscrapers, leveling land, putting cable and underground utilities in the ground and overhead, working on the railroads and highways, and the list goes on and on.

Some persons literally risk their lives working for only a little more than minimum wage in gas stations where the threat of armed robbery is very real and the gas station attendants are frequently killed in order for the criminal to have more time to getaway and to eliminate the witness. I worked in a gas station for about two years, and I was robbed by armed robbers three times. I barely made enough money in this gas station to pay a few of my bills, and I now realize I was literally risking my life every evening when I went to work. I once worked putting cable in the ground for about five years. I installed cable television cable for almost 2 years, and I installed power cable for about three years. I was a foreman in charge of a crew when I installed power cable, and the job was particularly demanding and frequently dangerous. The dangers that existed while I installed underground cable ranged from overturning the trencher while trenching on an embankment, stepping into a hole, falling off of the truck, being bitten by snakes or dogs, to being electrocuted while dealing with live lines and working inside live transformers.

When I installed cable television and power cables, I was a very young man in his early twenties. And, I was Baptized but not yet a born-again believing Christian. Nevertheless, God watched over me and kept me safe from harm as he promises in Psalm 121:5-6. You see, God's faithfulness to us is very great, and his faithfulness is on a scale that we don't quite comprehend and can't really understand. God is completely and thoroughly faithful. I was not saved when I did this difficult and dangerous underground construction work putting cable in the ground, but God watched over me every day and helped me to get my work done and kept me from getting seriously injured. When I think back at how difficult some of the jobs were, I know it was only with God's help that I was able to accomplish the task and get the power line installed. Nature can be very stubborn when you are trying to put something manmade, a cable, in ground that has never been disturbed. And, the resistance of hard ground, tree roots, underground water and streams, and other natural obstacles are symbolic of the obstacles we face in our sinful secular society within which we Christians try to live holy lives and let our lights shine for Christ and the glory of God. Worldly and sinful forces will try to intercept and impede our progress, but we have the assurance of God's presence and protection as we continue our journey. And, we know that we can do all things through Christ as he promises to be with us always and to give us his strength. (Matthew 28:20, Philippians 4:13)

The way God watched over me way back before I trusted in him is what we Wesleyan Christians call Prevenient Grace. This is the grace of God that comes to us before we accept Christ and trust in his atoning work at the cross and experience Justifying Grace. Then, as we obey Jesus' Great Commandments, pray, read the Bible, worship in church, and serve in our ministries, we grow in what we Wesleyan Christians call Sanctifying Grace. When we our justified at our conversions, God declares us "not guilty" of our sins, and as we obey God and his Word, and grow in our love for God and neighbor, we experience sanctification and holiness. Nevertheless, for purposes of this section of Psalm 121, it is Prevenient Grace, the grace that comes before our salvation experience, that points to the radical and amazing faithfulness and love of our heavenly Father. He loves us way before we love him as the apostle John points out in 1 John 4:19 where he says: "We love him, because he first loved us."

In Lamentations 3:21-26, the major prophet Jeremiah speaks of God's great faithfulness by stating:

> This I recall to my mind, therefore have I hope. It is of the Lord's mercies that we are not consumed, because his compassions fail not. They are new every morning: great is thy faithfulness. The Lord is my portion, saith my soul; therefore will I hope in him. The Lord is good unto them that wait for him, to the soul that seeketh him. It is good that a man should both

hope and quietly wait for the salvation of the Lord.

God is faithful, and he never tells us lies. This is very refreshing and comforting as we make our way through this world which is filled with fakes, lies, and hypocrisy. God's faithfulness is unrelenting and unwavering. God is completely faithful and dependable unlike any person, and he never stops watching over and caring for us. The Psalmist says in Psalm 121:5 that "…the Lord is thy shade upon thy right hand." This means that God watches over us in our work. Our right hand is symbolic of our hand of power and strength just as God's right hand symbolizes his strength and power throughout the Bible. God hovers over us, and we spend our days and nights within the comfort and protection of his shade. A shadow is only present when there is something very real and very present that casts the shadow. As we use our strengths, gifts, abilities, and talents in the world to work and earn a living, vv. 5-6 say we Christians who trust in him are under his shade and "The sun shall not smite [us] by day, nor the moon by night" (Psalm 121:6). Whether we do our work in the day or at night, we always have our heavenly Father watching over us and fulfilling his promises:

> ...that neither death, nor life, nor angels, nor principalities, nor powers, nor things present, nor things to come. Nor height, nor depth, nor any other creature, shall be able to separate us from the love of God, which is in Christ Jesus our Lord.
> (Romans 8:38-39)

God's Great Faithfulness, Tragedy, Suffering, and Romans 8:28

In v. 6, the Psalmist says: "The sun shall not smite thee by day, nor the moon by night" (Psalm

121:6). This means that God protects those who trust in him both day and night. In other words, God cares for and protects us Christians 24 hours a day. Now, this obviously prompts the question as to what happened to the Christians who have encountered great tragedy, bodily harm, horrific diseases, fatal car accidents, been victims of crime and murder, or have been burned in the fires of martyrdom or crucified on crosses like the apostle Peter and our Savior Jesus? Did God forsake them? Are their terrible fates and horrific experiences proof that Psalm 121:6 is not true? Did the sun smite them in the day or did the moon smite them at night?

Absolutely not! The fact that Christians encounter pain and suffering and tragedy in this life does not mean that God has forsaken them. Just because something bad happens to a person doesn't mean that God forsook them. God has the great ability to protect those who trust in him from the terrible events that actually happen to them. The Christian who has to go to prison for ten years will be protected from the lasting effects of incarceration. The Christian who is diagnosed and suffers with cancer or some other terrible disease will be protected by God from the lasting effects of the disease. The Christian who is murdered or burnt in the fires of martyrdom will be protected and kept from the lasting effects of death. Tragedy, disease, crime, and murder may assault us Christians, but these events will not overtake us. In 1 Corinthians 15:54-57, the apostle Paul highlights how we are victorious over death by stating:

> So when this corruptible shall have put on incorruption, and this mortal shall have put on immortality, then shall be

> brought to pass the saying that is written, Death is swallowed up in victory. O death, where is thy sting? O grave, where is thy victory? The sting of death is sin; and the strength of sin is the law. But thanks be to God, which giveth us the victory through our Lord Jesus Christ.

Here, St. Paul points to the victory we have in Jesus, and it is victory over the greatest enemy we will ever face which is death. Yes, we will probably face death one day unless Jesus returns during our lifetimes. However, we will experience bodily death, but death will not take hold of us or keep us in its grip. We have victory over death in and through our Lord Jesus Christ. Jesus points this out in many places in the Gospels as he does while comforting Martha in John 11:25-26 by declaring:

> ...I am the resurrection, and the life: he that believeth in me, though he were dead, yet shall he live: And whosoever

liveth and believeth in me shall never die. Believest thou this?

In Christ, the Christian has complete victory over the two greatest threats to his or her eternal existence which are sin and the wages or earned payment for sin which is death. (Romans 6:23) Death when spoken of in this context means the eternal cessation of existence which is not a reality or the eternal existence in a place where God is experientially not which is the placed inhabited by those who are eternally lost. The Christian never stops living, and he or she spends eternity in the place where God is which is heaven. Therefore, the great threats have been defeated by Christ at the cross, and we are cleansed from sin by the blood of Christ which makes us fit for heaven and able to spend eternity around God's throne worshiping God forever with all the others who have been redeemed and reconciled to God. (Revelation 5:1-14, 2 Corinthians 5:16-21)

When we pray the Lord's Prayer, one of the things we pray for is our daily bread as we pray: "Give us this day our daily bread" (Matthew 6:11). Our daily bread consists of many things other than just food and water. Yes, we pray and ask God to provide our food and drink for the day, but we are also asking God to provide many other things that we need to remain not only physically healthy but spiritually healthy also. And, the main thing we need to make it through each day is God. We need God to be with us as we make our journey through life. We need God to help us as we go through days of disappointment and despair. God is our daily bread. In and through him, we are more than conquerors, and we can do all things. (Romans 8:37, Philippians 4:13) Our assurance that God is with us gives us the strength and hope to endure and to press on through days and months or even years of trial and difficulty.

In Psalm 23:4, the Psalmist emphasizes this by stating: "Yea, though I walk through the valley of the shadow of death, I will fear no evil: for thou art with me; thy rod and thy staff they comfort me." In my doctoral dissertation on Psalm 23, I argued that Verse 4 of Psalm 23 is the eye of the wonderful spiritual hurricane we Christians know and love which is Psalm 23. And, more specifically, these five words are the center of that eye: "…for thou art with me;…" (Psalm 23:4) These five words represent the place of calm in the midst of our lives. These five words are the place where we are grounded, kept, saved, sanctified, and liberated. These five words are heaven and eternity with the God who is our Daily Bread. These five words are the reason we have hope in the midst of horror, life in the midst of death, wellness in the midst of disease, fullness in the midst of hunger, and quenching in the midst of thirst. In Christ, bleeding and dying on the cross, we have all things, and we can do all things. This is the true meaning of Psalm 23:1 where the Psalmist triumphantly proclaims: "The Lord is my shepherd; I shall not want." And, this is what Paul celebrates in Romans 8:31-32 where he proclaims:

> What shall we then say to these things? If God be for us, who can be against us? He that spared not his own Son, but delivered him up for us all, how shall he not with him also freely give us all things?

When we Christians face tragedy and heartache in our lives, we find great comfort in Paul's magnificent words in Romans 8:28. In this famous and frequently quoted and referenced verse of Scripture, the apostle Paul proclaims: "And we know that all things work together for good to them that love God, to them who are the called according to his purpose" (Romans 8:28). This powerful verse holds a great promise for the "obedient" Christian disciple. In other words, it holds a great promise, but it is a "conditional" promise. The "obedient" Christian disciple can rest in the glorious truth that all things will work together for his or her good, but the "disobedient" Christian "believer" cannot. There is a great difference between being an "obedient" Christian disciple and a "disobedient" Christian believer. The former is a radical force for good and contributor to the expansion of his Lord's kingdom on earth. The latter still does his own thing and bends his Christianity in directions that fulfill his own personal goals, preferences, and agendas. The former loves Jesus enough to obey him as Lord and is definitely saved and heaven bound. The latter may or may not be saved and may be continuing to make daily decisions based on his or her personal agenda and could be destined to an eternity separated from God.

The promises of Psalm 121:5-6 and Romans 8:28 only apply to "obedient" Christian disciples who meet the two conditions of Romans 8:28 and love God and are striving to answer his call on their lives. In order for the Christian to be able to take comfort in the fact that all things work together for his or her good, he or she must be loving God by obeying Jesus' Great Commandments to love God and all persons. And, he or she must be daily striving to answer God's call and to do God's will on a daily basis and in the entirety of his or her life and ministry. When these two conditions are met, when we love God and obey his Great Commandments, and we daily answer his call on our lives and live our lives for him, we can take great solace, comfort, and hope in the Biblical truth of Romans 8:28. We can know that all things, even the worst and most tragic events, in our lives will, in God's great oversight and providential care, work together for our good in our lives and ministries.

As long as we love God by obeying his Great Commandments that we love God and each other, and we daily strive to answer his call on our lives by using our gifts for his glory and the expansion of his

Son's kingdom, we can also take great comfort and have wonderful assurance that:

> The Lord is thy keeper: the Lord is thy shade upon thy right hand. The sun shall not smite thee by day, nor the moon by night.
> (Psalm 121:5-6)

As we go about our days using our right hands to love God and others, and to daily answer God's call on our lives, we can know that God will indeed be the "...shade upon [our] right hand. [and that the] sun shall not smite [us] by day, nor the moon by night" (Psalm 121:5-6).

Yes, we "obedient" Christian disciples do encounter tragedy, crime, natural disasters, heartbreak, disease, grief, pain, and suffering, but we do it knowing that God is still in charge and all is or will ultimately be well. And, in those fleeting moments when we question God's management skills or briefly think he may have stopped steering the ship, we look at the cross which sits on our altars, towers on top of our steeples, and hangs around our necks, and we know that God is for us, and he keeps all of his promises, even when he is the One who suffers the most because he was "...oppressed and was afflicted, yet he opened not his mouth: he [was] brought as a lamb to the slaughter, and as a sheep before her shearers is dumb, so he [opened] not his mouth" (Isaiah 53:7, Please see Isaiah 53:1-12).

PART IV – PSALM 121:7-8

Chapter 4 – Psalm 121:7-8

"The Lord shall preserve thee from all evil: he shall preserve thy soul. The Lord shall preserve thy going out and thy coming in from this time forth, and even for evermore."

Delivered from Evil by the Power of a Present God

In the last two verses of Psalm 121, we are reminded that God protects us from evil and cares for and protects our souls. In v. 7, the Psalmist says: "The Lord shall preserve thee from all evil: he shall preserve thy soul" (Psalm 121:7). The two promises contained in v. 7 are wonderful and precious promises that those who trust in Christ can stand upon. In this world and the culture we live in, we encounter much deception, lies, disloyalty, and other people, places, and things that are fake and disingenuous. I celebrate the 28th Anniversary of my Conversion next month, and I can personally attest to the great and unwavering faithfulness of Jesus Christ. It is indeed true that he is faithful, and he keeps his promises. He has never abandoned me, lied to me, or misled me. He always tells me the truth through his Word both written and proclaimed, and I am only a minister of the Gospel today because he called, equipped, educated, and ordained me a minister in his holy church. As a Christian for 28 years now, I can assure you that Jesus Christ will never let you down. He will make you greater than you ever thought you could be, and he may even call you to make Christian history as you "obediently" live out the calling he places on your life. As you live your life honoring God and obeying Jesus by loving God and neighbor, you begin to understand what the apostle Paul speaks of in Ephesians 3:20 where he says Jesus "…is able to do exceeding abundantly above all that we ask or think, according to the power that worketh in us."

Now, even though God is faithful and Jesus keeps his promises, the Christian life is not always easy. We Christians encounter pain, suffering, disappointment, disease, tragedy, and death just like everyone else does. However, we encounter these things with a very strong awareness of the presence of God with us and this gives us hope. The only "completely" hopeless situation would be a situation involving us being in a place where God is not and our hope in him did not exist. One may say that this is easy for me to say as I type this chapter of my book on Psalm 121 in the comfort of my parsonage, on a Tuesday evening, after having a delicious supper and doing my job as a pastor all day, which I love and enjoy very much. However, I too have encountered suffering at various times in my life. I have dealt with sickness, pain, disappointment, and loss, but I have never, since my conversion 28 years ago, been in a situation where I didn't know God was near and had hope because of his presence, power, and promises.

When the apostle Paul describes the glorious event we call the Rapture, which is the glorious day of our Lord's appearing, St. Paul is answering a question the Thessalonians have sent to him about how they are to handle and deal with the death of their fellow Christians within the Christian community at Thessalonica. Although it is a powerful passage of Scripture, very worthy of me writing an entire book or two on it alone, I quote just v. 13 of 1 Thessalonians 4:13-18. Paul introduces this passage about the Rapture of the church by stating: "But I would not have you to be ignorant brethren, concerning them which are asleep, that ye sorrow not, even as others which have no hope" (1 Thessalonians 4:13). Then, Paul goes on to describe the events of the Rapture of the church as the dead in Christ rise first, and we are "...caught up together with them in the clouds, to meet the Lord in the air: and so shall we ever be with the Lord" (1 Thessalonians 4:13-18). I frequently read this verse, v. 13, when I as a pastor visit the home of someone who has lost a loved one. Oftentimes, I read just v. 13 from this passage and then some other passages, and I usually close the visit with prayer. I read v. 13 of 1 Thessalonians 4:13-18 because it acknowledges that we Christians do indeed grieve. We grieve and hurt when we lose a loved one just like everyone else. However, we do not grieve like those who don't know God. We do not grieve and have sorrow like unbelievers who have no relationship with the God who "…created the heaven and the earth" (Genesis 1:1). We do not grieve like those who have no hope in God and the earth and heaven he created. Yes, we grieve, but we grieve with hope in our faithful, loving, and giving God. We know that he is with us in the darkest times of our lives and during those times of darkness, when we see darkness all around us, we stare into God's light as the Psalmist proclaims: "For with thee is the fountain of life: in thy light shall we see light" (Psalm 36:9).

Just as we Christians are not shielded from grief sorrow, and death, we are also not completely shielded from evil and wickedness. Many great Christians are famous martyrs who gave their lives for Christ at the hands of the wicked, and there are many more whose names may only be known to Christ who suffered and died as they were martyred with the praises of Christ on their lips. So, as we read in Psalm 121:7, that: "The Lord shall preserve thee from all evil: he shall preserve thy soul....," we give God thanks and praise that, although we do encounter evil, and we are sometimes injured by evil, and we could even one day be martyred at the hands of evil men, we can trust in this great promise from our loving and faithful God that he will preserve us and keep us from evil, and he will preserve and keep our souls. (Psalm 121:7). In other words, yes, we will encounter evil in this world, and we will sometimes be harmed or injured by it, but it will not keep us, and it will not hold us. Evil cannot hold and keep us in its clutches because we are in the hands of our Lord and Savior, Jesus Christ, and he promises us that:

> My sheep hear my voice, and I know them, and they follow me: And I give unto them eternal life; and they shall never perish, neither shall any man pluck them out of my hand. My Father, which gave them me, is greater than all; and no man is able to pluck them out of my Father's hand. I and my Father are one.
> (John 10:27-30)

In the Lord's Prayer, we pray: "And lead us not into temptation, but deliver us from evil:…" (Matthew 6:12) This particular petition in the Lord's Prayer has been misunderstood by many, and the source of some confusion for some, because it initially appears that we are praying for God not to lead, direct, or guide us into temptation that may result in sin. However, God never "leads" us into sin. When we sin, it is our doing and our choice. In order for sin to be sin, we must choose it. Of course, I am speaking here of very serious "sins of commission" like hatred, murder, lust, adultery, coveting, and stealing.

We can never claim that God is at fault for the serious sins we commit in our lives. God is not at fault. We are at fault, and our sins that separate us from God, and bring about misery in our lives and the lives of those around us, are our own. The apostle James highlights this in James 1:12-16 where he proclaims:

> Blessed is the man that endureth temptation: for when he is tried, he shall receive the crown of life, which the Lord hath promised to them that love him. Let no man say when he is tempted, I am tempted of God: for God cannot be tempted with evil, neither tempteth he any man: But every man is tempted, when he is drawn away of his own lust, and enticed. Then when lust hath conceived, it bringeth forth sin:

and sin, when it is finished, bringeth forth death. Do not err, my beloved brethren.

So, when we pray and ask God not to lead us into temptation, we are not implying that he leads us into temptation, but we are asking him to lead us "…in the paths of righteousness for his name's sake" (Psalm 23:3). We are simply asking for God's presence and power to be with us in times of temptation so that we can say "no" to temptation and say "yes" to God when temptation comes our way. This is in part what the apostle Paul speaks of in Romans 6:12-14 where he states:

> Let not sin therefore reign in your mortal body, that ye should obey it in the lusts thereof. Neither yield ye your members as instruments of unrighteousness unto sin: but yield yourselves unto God, as those that are alive from the dead, and your members as instruments of righteousness unto God. For sin shall not have dominion

over you: for ye are not under the law, but under grace.

As we consistently resist the small and big temptations that come our way, and we consistently choose God's way instead of the way of this world or our flesh, we grow in Sanctifying Grace and become holier women and men of God. Then, we see how v. 7 of Psalm 121 becomes a visible and tangible reality in our lives. Instead of holiness taking a back seat in our lives, and leaving us behind and always playing catch up, sin takes a back seat and is unable to effect how the driver, the Holy Spirit, guides and directs us along this long and magnificent road we call life.

Indeed, the promise of Psalm 121:7 is literally true in the life of the "obedient" Christian disciple who daily and consistently obeys God's

Commandments and chooses to do things God's way. In Psalm 121:7, the Psalmist says "The Lord shall preserve thee from all evil: he shall preserve thy soul." When we are the ones who consistently and habitually do things God's way, and share God's love with the world, we will be able to see that God protects us from evil and protects our souls. Sure, evil will attack us from time to time. We will face hardship, rejection, persecution, and some of us will face martyrdom, but God will always protect and preserve us from the lasting effects of evil and wickedness. Evil men and women may separate our heads from our bodies as we kneel and pray to our Savior, but they will never separate our souls from the loving, giving, very present, and very real, nail-scarred hands of our Savior, Jesus Christ, who tells us: "…I am the bread of life: he that cometh to me shall never hunger; and he that believeth on me shall never thirst" (John 6:35).

God's Presence, Power, Provision, and Protection: God as Father and Friend

One of God's most wonderful attributes is his great faithfulness to those who trust in his Son our Lord Jesus Christ. Oftentimes, we Christians look back over our lives, and we are amazed at how faithful God is. In a world filled with those who will abandon you at the drop of a hat, God's faithfulness is an amazing blessing. Indeed, God loves all people, and Jesus' blood shed at the cross is more than enough to atone for the sins of all persons. However, only those who confess with their mouths and believe with their hearts, that Jesus is Savior and Lord, will be saved and enjoy the blessing of having their sin-debt paid and the joy of being reconciled to God. (Romans 10:9-10, 2 Corinthians 5:16-21) Hundreds of years before the birth of Christ, God speaks of his great love for us through the major prophet Jeremiah "…saying, Yea, I have loved thee with an everlasting love: therefore with lovingkindness have I drawn thee" (Jeremiah 31:3). By his grace, God draws us to himself, and we answer and are saved, restored, and recreated. Then, he provides the grace we need, through the power and the presence of the Holy Spirit, for us to stay on the right path that ultimately leads us to heaven.

We pray and ask God to provide us with guidance, and the ability to stay in the "narrow way" that leads to life, (Matthew 7:13-14) in the Lord's Prayer when we pray: "Give us this day our daily bread:" (Matthew 6:11) We don't just need physical food and water in order to walk, grow, endure, and enjoy the wonderful gift of life, but we also need spiritual bread and spiritual water. We need God's Word written and proclaimed, and we need worship in Christ's holy church. We need the Sacrament of Holy Communion and to break bread and drink juice together as we remind ourselves that our Savior loves, died, and rose again for each one of us and for all of us. We need to experience the presence and power of God in our lives, ministries, and marriages as we are acutely aware that life is indeed God's great gift as we get to live in his kingdom here on earth and forever with him in heaven.

As we obey our Lord's Great Commandments by loving God and each other, and by doing loving things for God and others, we come to know the magnificent joy and elation that comes from living a life with God as our Father and Jesus as our Friend who lives and moves in our hearts and lives, through the presence and power of the Holy Spirit. We pray for this in the Lord's Prayer as we pray: "Thy kingdom come. Thy will be done in earth, as it is in heaven" (Matthew 6:10). This is the miraculous transformation that God brings about in the homes, hearts, lives, and ministries of those who trust in Jesus as Savior and consistently and joyfully obey him as Lord.

We "obedient" Christians are the ones who experience God as faithful Father and friend. We "obedient" Christians are the ones who experience the kingdom of heaven here on earth way before we experience for all of eternity when we get to heaven, and we "obedient" Christians are the ones who know and experience God's protection and provision as we see that: "The Lord shall preserve [our] going out and [our] coming in from this time forth, and even for evermore" (Psalm 121:8). We will gladly pass on the temporary and fleeting things of this world which offer fulfillment but instead deliver frustration, heartbreak, and disappointment. We are being shaped for eternity with God, and we have developed a taste for the most wonderful things the universe has to offer which includes love and friendship with God, love for our families, friends, and enemies, and a desire and yearning to spread the Good News of Jesus Christ so more sinners can be rescued from this fake and fallen world and begin to experience what it means for "...goodness and mercy [to] follow [them] all the days of [their lives]: and [to] dwell in the house of the Lord for ever" (Psalm 23:6).

We "obedient" Christians know that every day is a miracle and a great gift from God, and we have the opportunity to lead a lost sinner to Christ everyday as we go out and come back in to the homes and families and worshipping communities that God has blessed us to be a part of. We Christians must care for the lost, and we Christians must witness to the lost because we may be the only Bible that a person ever reads. We must "show" them God's love instead of just telling them we love them as we are "…doers of the word, and not hearers only, deceiving [our] own selves" (James 1:22). We Christians must love God, each other, our enemies, and the lost in a way that reflects that we are truly friends of the Lord who says in John 15:14: "Ye are my friends, if ye do whatsoever I command you."

Printed in Great Britain
by Amazon